# MANDALA SEASONS
## ADULT COLORING BOOK

## FRUIT & FLOWERS
### BOOK 3

### PRODUCED BY

Maya Necalli

&

art therapy designs

Copyright © 2016 by Maya Necalli
All rights reserved.

**Images may not be replicated or reproduced.**

No part of this publication may be reproduced, transmitted or circulated in any form without permission in writing from the copyright owner.

ISBN: 1539526631
ISBN-13: 978-1539526636

Cover design by Art Therapy Designs.

First Edition: October 2016

# INTRODUCTION

Art Therapy Designs presents unique theme-based mandala collections inspired by various cultures and the natural world. This is the third book in the *Mandala Seasons: Fruit & Flowers* series.

This coloring book contains 45 floral patterns presented as single-sided pages to help preserve each illustration.

The designs range from easy to high difficulty.

Feel free to begin wherever you'd like!

Coloring is a form of art therapy, a creative calming technique that aids in de-stressing and relaxation.

Our therapeutic activity book is designed for grownups but suitable for all advanced children and teens.

Enjoy!

NOTE: Cover image can be found at the beginning.

# SPECIAL OFFERS

Visit our Facebook page to get free designs and find out when new coloring books are available!

Go to: www.facebook.com/ArtTherapyDesigns

You can also win freebies and keep up with new releases by joining our newsletter (see Facebook page).

# FINAL WORD

Thank you for your purchase!

More coloring books coming soon from Art Therapy Designs.

See our Facebook page for updates and giveaways!

Visit: www.facebook.com/ArtTherapyDesigns

www.ingramcontent.com/pod-product-compliance
Lightning Source LLC
Chambersburg PA
CBHW080713190526
45169CB00006B/2363